MACHINE MANIA

RESCUE VEHICLES

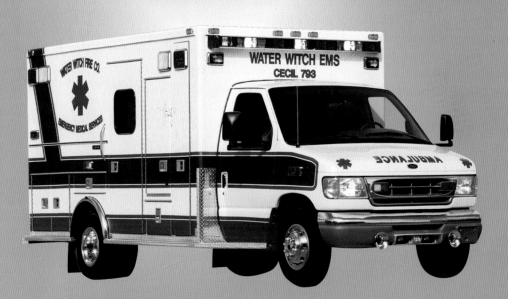

Frances Ridley

Copyright © ticktock Entertainment Ltd 2007
First published in Great Britain in 2007 by ticktock Media Ltd.,
Unit 2, Orchard Business Centre, North Farm Road,
Tunbridge Wells, Kent, TN2 3XF

ticktock project editor: Julia Adams
ticktock project designer: Emma Randall

We would like to thank: Alix Wood.

ISBN 978 1 84696 564 7

Printed in China

Picture credits:
b=bottom; c=centre; t=top; r=right; l=left
Alamy: 2b, 22-23c; Bronto: 6-7c, 7tl; Check-6 Images: 12-13c, 13tl; Jane's Defence Weekly: 16-
17c; Oshkosh: 2t, 4-5c, 5t, 8-9c, b/c: cr; Perry Slingsby Systems: 20-21c; Robinson Helicopters:
10-11c, 11tl; Sylvia Corday Photo Library: 21tl; US Coastguard: 14bl, 14-15c, 17tr, 18-19c, 19tr, b/c: cl

Every effort has been made to trace the copyright holders,
and we apologise in advance for any unintentional omissions.
We would be pleased to insert the appropriate acknowledgements
in any subsequent edition of this publication.

Contents

Striker 4500 4

Bronto Skylift Fire Engine............................ 6

Medtec Saturn Ambulance 8

R44 Helicopter 10

Super Huey Helicopter 12

P-3 Orion Airtanker.................................... 14

Marine Protector.. 16

HH-6OJ Jayhawk....................................... 18

LR5 and LR7 Rescue Submersibles 20

Hagglunds BV206...................................... 22

Glossary 24

Striker 4500

The Striker is a huge fire engine. It fights airport fires with water and **foam**. It holds as much water as nine normal fire engines!

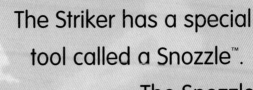

The Striker has a special tool called a Snozzle™. The Snozzle™ makes a hole in a burning plane.

It puts a camera through to see where the fire is. Then it shoots foam through to put the fire out.

Bronto Skylift Fire Engine

The Bronto Skylift fights fires in very tall buildings. Its thick hose shoots 3,800 litres of water a minute.

The Skylift reaches higher than any other fire engine. It can reach the 33rd floor of a **skyscraper**. It lifts the firefighters up on a platform. They rescue people trapped inside.

This Skylift can reach 72 metres in the air. It can carry people down safely.

Medtec Saturn Ambulance

Ambulances take sick people to hospital. The flashing lights warn traffic to get out of the way.

The Saturn has two back doors. There is lots of room to load **stretchers** on and off.

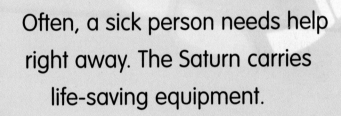

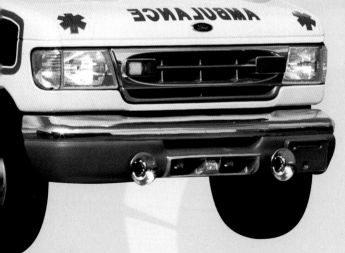

Often, a sick person needs help right away. The Saturn carries life-saving equipment. The equipment needs electricity. The electricity comes from a **battery pack**.

R44 Helicopter

The R44 is a police helicopter. The police can see everything that happens on the ground. They can chase criminals who try to escape.

Special equipment helps the police to do their work. The R44 has a **search light**, a **siren** and a **loud speaker**. It also has a special camera that works at night.

Super Huey Helicopter

The Super Huey used to be an army helicopter. Now it fights forest fires.

The Super Huey is large for a helicopter. It carries nine crew and their firefighting equipment.

FIRE N491DF CDF

The Super Huey
can fill up its
water tank from
a river or lake.
The water is
sucked up through
a hose. It can carry 916 litres
of water and **foam**.

P-3 Orion Airtanker

The P-3 Orion Airtanker used to be a spy plane. Now, it fights forest fires. It's named after a group of stars called 'Orion'.

The P-3 has a huge tank of **fire retardant** under its body. The plane drops the fire retardant in a straight line. The fire can't spread over this line.

Marine Protector

The Marine Protector is a patrol boat. It keeps the coast safe.

The Marine Protector is fast and strong. Its top speed is 45 km/h. It can go out into rough seas. It chases criminals and rescues people.

U. S. COAST GUARD

The **pilot house** has lots of windows. The crew can see in all directions. The crew's special equipment is kept here, too.

HH-6OJ Jayhawk

The Jayhawk saves people who get into trouble at sea. It can carry 4 crew and 6 survivors. It travels at 257 km/h.

The pilot keeps the Jayhawk hovering in one place. It lowers a rescuer down on a line. The rescuer pulls the person out of the sea. The Jayhawk pulls them both up. It takes the survivor to hospital.

LR5 and LR7 Rescue Submersibles

Rescue **submersibles** rescue people trapped in **submarines**.

The rescue submersible goes underwater. It finds the submarine and fixes on to it. The trapped people move into the submersible.

The LR5 has been rescuing people for over 20 years.

The LR7 was launched in 2004. It can carry 21 people. 18 people can sit in the rescue **chamber** at the back.

Hagglunds BV206

The Hagglunds BV206 fights fires and rescues people. Its top speed is 51 km/h on roads and 3 km/h in the water.

It explores deserts and jungles. It can turn into an ambulance. It can even float!

The Hagglunds has special tracks. They can go over snow, ice, mud, grass or sand.

426 PERISHER VALLEY

NSW FIRE BRIGADES

Glossary

Battery pack   A supply of electricity that can be carried around.

Chamber   A room.

Fire retardant   A liquid dropped onto fires to stop them spreading.

Foam   Froth that you use to fight fires.

Loud speaker   A tool that makes your voice louder.

Search light   A lamp that can direct a very strong light in any direction.

Siren   A tool that makes a very loud, piercing noise.

Skyscraper   A very tall building.

Stretcher   A piece of cloth held by two poles that can carry sick and injured people.

Submarines   Underwater warships.

Submersibles   Boats that can go underwater.